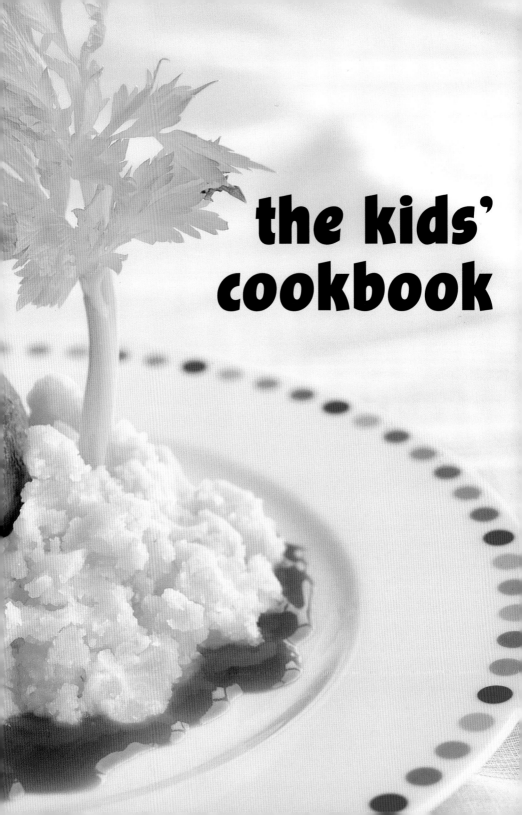

the kids' cookbook

This edition first published in 2006 by
Kyle Cathie Limited

Kyle Cathie Limited
122 Arlington Road
London NW1 7HP

ISBN (13-digit) 978 1 85626 626 0

Text copyright © 2005 Kyle Cathie Ltd
Photography copyright © 2005 Will Heap
Book design © 2005 Kyle Cathie Limited

Senior Editor Helen Woodhall
Designer Geoff Hayes
Photography Will Heap
Home Economist Angela Boggiano and Jenny White
Food Stylist Penny Markham
Indexer Alex Corrin
Production Sha Huxtable and Alice Holloway

Colour reproduction by Scanhouse
Printed and bound in China by C&C Offset Printers

With special thanks to Kate Arthur, Linda Bain, Nicola Donovan,
Amanda Fries, Sarah Lee and Kate McBain. Many thanks also to
Anna and Arthur for modelling for photographs.

With thanks and acknowledgement to all the recipe writers
whose talents have contributed to the creation of this book.

First published in Great Britain in 2005 by Kyle Cathie Limited for
Sainsbury's Supermarkets Limited

Kyle Cathie Limited
122 Arlington Road
London NW1 7HP
www.kylecathie.com

contents

happy cooking!

We believe that children of all ages can enjoy cooking and that food that's fun to make and eat can be healthy too. With this in mind and help from a whole team of kids, parents and food experts we've put together a collection of recipes especially for budding master chefs. While a grown up should always be on hand to help plenty of the recipes require very little or no cutting and cooking and so can be tackled by the youngest cooks. Other, more ambitious recipes are perfect for children who are keen to get stuck into 'real' cooking or helping to make a family meal.

How does the book work?

First check the 'egg' rating. One egg means simple, two eggs means a fair amount of preparation is required - for example chopping under adult supervision. The most challenging recipes are marked with three eggs. These are great recipes to cook together and will always include easy fun elements like spooning sauce or layering pasta sheets.

Every recipe is divided into two parts: 'what do I need?' and 'how do I do that?'. Before you start it's best to work through the list and get all the ingredients and utensils you need together in one place. 'How do I do that' then breaks the recipe down into numbered stages.

Please note some recipes, for example the wrap on page 26 will require some pre-preparation of ingredients, with the egg rating applying to the 'how do I do that?' section.

As a quick reference we've also included how many people the recipe serves, how long it takes to cook and some basic nutritional information as a guide.

In this book we aim to offer healthier food for kids that doesn't skimp on taste. We have brought together a selection of fun nutritious recipes that will keep your taste buds tingling! Good food gives us the energy and nutrients we need to keep us healthy. Choose here from delicious recipes that are based on the four main food groups - starchy foods, fruit and veg, dairy and meat, fish and alternatives. Choosing foods from the four main food groups will help to give the range of nutrients needed for a balanced diet. We've also included some favourite sweet treats and thirst busting drinks.

Please note, the eggs used in this book are medium sized. All spoon measurements for dry ingredients are heaped. 1 teaspoon = 5ml, 1 tablespoon = 15ml. Always use either metric or imperial measurements when following a recipe - never mix the two.

Top tips for successful cooking

Finally, before you get going here are some basic rules followed by all the best chefs.

1 Keep clean! Wash your hands before starting and wipe up any spills as you go.

2 Wear an apron or spare shirt while you cook - you're bound to get a bit messy!

3 If your hair is long make sure it's held or tied back - nobody likes hair in their soup!

4 Always keep raw food separate to ready to eat food - also use separate kitchen utensils / surfaces when preparing them (if you can't then make sure you wash the equipment thoroughly between use).

5 Always cook raw meat and fish thoroughly until it is piping hot and no pink colour remains.

6 Fruit and vegetables should always be washed before they are eaten or when used in recipes.

7 Be extra careful with anything that's sharp or hot. We recommend all junior chefs have a grown-up to hand to help with the tricky bits! If you do burn or cut yourself tell and adult straight away.
Never put a hot dish on a table covered with a tablecloth - a small child could pull off the cloth off taking the dish with it.

8 Never leave pan handles sticking out from the front of the cooker, they can easily be knocked.

9 Always use oven gloves when handling hot things - get a grown up to help take things out of the oven.

10 Never put a hot dish on a table covered with a tablecloth - a small child could pull the cloth off, taking the dish with it.

11 Always put any bowls or jugs or pans you are using on non-slip surfaces. If they are very hot make sure the surface is heat proof.

Now you're ready to get going - happy cooking!

what's for lunch?

lunchbox wrap

You'll have lunch all wrapped up with these fantastic flatbreads!

what do I need?

2 soft cheese triangles
1 tomato flatbread
1 carrot, peeled and grated
1 red pepper, deseeded, cut into thin strips
small piece cucumber, cut into thin strips
salt and freshly ground black pepper

You will also need a knife, a cheese grater, a bread knife and some cling film.

how do I do that?

1 Spread the cheese triangles over the tomato flatbread and sprinkle with the grated carrot.

2 Cut the flatbread in half and arrange the strips of red pepper and cucumber over both halves of the bread. Season with salt and pepper to taste.

3 Roll each half up to enclose the filling and wrap in a piece of cling film to hold it together and keep it moist before packing into a lunchbox.

chicken & pasta salad

Good for lunch at the weekend, or for a picnic on a sunny day.

what do I need?

250g (8oz) pasta such as fusilli tricolore
375g (13oz) cooked chicken breast, cubed
1 red pepper, finely cubed
4 salad onions, finely cubed
2 tablespoons freshly chopped coriander
3 tablespoons mayonnaise
salt and freshly ground black pepper

You will also need a large saucepan, a
colander, a large bowl, a sharp knife, kitchen
scissors, a mug and a small mixing bowl.

To chop herbs safely, put them in a mug and chop using kitchen scissors.

how do I do that?

1 Cook the pasta for approximately 10-15 minutes, following the instructions on the pack, drain it well, and place in the large bowl to cool down.

2 When the pasta is cool, add the chicken, pepper, salad onions and most of the coriander.

3 In the small bowl, mix together the mayonnaise and salt and pepper and then stir into the pasta mixture. Sprinkle the remaining coriander over the top and serve.

Pasta should be cooked until it is 'al dente' which means cooked through, without being overcooked. It should still have a slight 'bite' when you chomp it rather than being mushy and too soft.

fun fish cakes

These fish-shaped treats are bursting with goodness!

what do I need?

425g (14oz) potatoes, peeled and chopped
1 tablespoon half-fat spread or butter
2 tablespoons semi-skimmed milk
500g (1lb) cooked white fish fillets, skinned and flaked,
   eg cod, coley or haddock
2 medium-size eggs, hard-boiled and chopped
1 tablespoon fresh parsley, chopped
1 tablespoon flour
salt and freshly ground black pepper

For the breadcrumb coating:
2 medium-size eggs, beaten
150g (5oz) wholemeal breadcrumbs

tomato slices
a few salad leaves
fresh parsley, or dill sprigs

You will also need a potato peeler, a sharp knife, a large saucepan,
a large mixing bowl, a potato masher, 2 baking trays and 2
shallow bowls.

how do I do that?

1 Cook the potatoes in boiling lightly salted water for about
15 minutes until tender. Drain the potatoes and put them in the
large bowl.

2 Mash the potatoes with the half-fat spread or butter and milk. Add salt and pepper. Add the cooked fish, hard-boiled eggs and parsley and mix well.

3 Divide the mixture into 12 and form into simple fish shapes using well-floured hands. Place on the baking tray and put in the fridge for at least 10 minutes.

4 Prepare 2 shallow bowls: put the beaten egg into one bowl and the breadcrumbs into the other. Dip each fish shape in the beaten egg and then into the breadcrumbs.

5 Grill the shapes under a preheated moderate grill for 5 minutes each side, or until golden brown and heated through. Carefully remove using oven gloves and serve garnished with tomato slices, salad leaves and parsley or dill.

apple and cheese toasties

30 mins prep & cook time

serves 4

285 cals per serving

16g fat per serving

As easy to make as plain cheese on toast, but more interesting and just as tasty!

what do I need?

2 red-skinned dessert apples
4 thick slices wholemeal bread
10g (¹/₂oz) butter, softened
150g (5oz) Cheddar, Cheshire or Emmental cheese, grated
1 teaspoon paprika
2 sage leaves, finely chopped

You will also need a cheese grater, a sharp knife and oven gloves.

how do I do that?

1 Cut the apples into quarters, remove the cores and slice the apples finely.

2 Heat the grill to the highest setting. Toast the bread on one side under the grill.

3 Turn the bread over, butter the untoasted side and arrange the apple slices on top. Sprinkle with the cheese, a pinch of paprika and the sage.

4 Grill for 2-3 minutes until the cheese melts and the apple cooks through. Carefully remove using the oven gloves, and serve.

fun tortilla wraps

A fun and healthy do-it-yourself dinner!

what do I need?

6 flour tortillas
100g (3¹/₂oz) wafer-thin ham
200g (7oz) sliced, cooked chicken nuggets or sausages
1 jar tomato salsa
1 punnet cherry tomatoes
1 iceberg lettuce, shredded
1 cucumber, cut into sticks
2 carrots, peeled and grated
175g (6oz) Cheddar or Emmental cheese, grated
6 soft cheese triangles
mayonnaise

You will also need a knife, a cheese grater, 6 bowls and oven gloves.

how do I do that?

1 Warm the tortillas in the microwave for 1 minute on full power, or wrap them in foil and place in a preheated oven at 180°C/350°F/gas mark 4 for 5 minutes. Carefully remove using oven gloves.

2 Put all the other ingredients in bowls and place them on the table. Spread each tortilla with soft cheese and pile the rest of the ingredients on top. Roll up and eat!

muffin pizza faces

These fun pizzas are great for picnics or packed in your lunchbox.

what do I need?

prep & cook time · serves 4 · 167 cals per serving · 9g fat per serving

2 white muffins, split in half
2 tablespoons tomato pizza sauce
50g (2oz) mild Cheddar cheese, grated
4 slices red Leicester cheese
1 small green pepper, deseeded
1 small red pepper, deseeded
4 pitted black olives

You will also need a sharp knife, a cheese grater, a baking tray and oven gloves.

how do I do that?

1 Preheat the oven to 190°C/375°F/gas mark 5.

2 Place the muffin halves, cut side up, on the baking tray. Spread some pizza sauce on each one and sprinkle grated Cheddar on top.

3 Carefully cut out 8 small circles from the red Leicester and place at the top of the muffins to resemble ears. Cut 8 small circles from the green pepper to resemble eyes. Cut 8 smiley mouths and tongues from the red pepper. Arrange the olives in the centre as noses.

4 Place in the preheated oven for 10-12 minutes until the cheese is melted and golden. Carefully remove using oven gloves and serve straight away.

If you want to take these pizzas on a picnic, cook them first, then allow them to cool completely. Pack them in a container with a sheet of greaseproof paper between each pizza to help them keep their shape on the way to the picnic.

fruity chicken salad

30 mins
prep & cook time

serves 2

178 cals
per serving

7g fat
per serving

This salad is great on its own, as a sandwich filling, with tortilla wraps or as a tasty topping for baked potatoes.

what do I need?

100g (3½oz) cooked chicken breast, cut into bite-sized pieces
2 salad onions, finely chopped
1 punnet seedless white grapes, halved
100g (3½oz) pineapple, fresh or canned, cut into bite-sized pieces
  and/or 1 small mango, peeled and cubed
1 tablespoon mayonnaise

You will also need a sharp knife, a large bowl and a wooden spoon.

how do I do that?

1 Place the cooked chicken in the large bowl with the salad onions, grapes, pineapple, mango, if using, and mayonnaise.

2 Mix together. Serve with pitta bread, tortilla wraps, crusty bread or baked potatoes.

If you use a mango, make sure it is ripe, otherwise it will not taste as sweet. A ripe mango has a sweet smell and feels slightly soft when you press it lightly with your thumb.

caterpillar sandwich

This creepy crawly sandwich is great for parties.

what do I need?

9 slices white bread
9 slices wholemeal or granary bread
25g (1oz) butter or margarine
6 cheese slices
1/2 tablespoon Marmite
1/2 x 185g (6¹/₂oz) can tuna steak in brine, drained
1-2 tablespoons mayonnaise
125g (4oz) mixed salad or shredded lettuce leaves, washed
1 small red pepper, washed, deseeded and cut into thin strips,
  keeping a small piece to make 2 eyes and a mouth
a few Twiglets to garnish

You will also need a pastry cutter, a knife, a large serving plate and 3 cocktail sticks.

30 mins — prep time

serves 6

232 cals — per serving

9g fat — per serving

how do I do that?

1 Use the pastry cutter to cut 2 rounds from each slice of bread. Spread thinly on one side with the butter or margarine.

2 Fill 6 sandwiches with cheese slices and 6 with Marmite. Mix together the tuna and mayonnaise and use to fill the remaining 6 sandwich rounds.

3 Arrange the salad on the large plate or a chopping board covered with foil. Place the sandwiches on the leaves in a line, alternating the brown and white bread to form the caterpillar's body.

4 Arrange the pepper strips by the sides of the caterpillar as legs. Press 2 Twiglets into the top of the front sandwich to make antennae.

5 Cut a small mouth and 2 eyes from the red pepper you have kept aside. Arrange on the front sandwich, securing with cocktail sticks. (Make sure you remove the cocktail sticks before eating).

If you don't have a pastry cutter, use a drinking glass or mug instead.

what's for tea?

crunchy cauliflower & macaroni

Everyone will love this crunchy-topped pasta recipe.

what do I need?

30 mins — prep & cook time

serves 4

379 cals — per serving

15g fat — per serving

1 cauliflower, divided into small florets
125g (4oz) quick-cook macaroni
25g (1oz) butter
125g (4oz) mushrooms, sliced
295g (10oz) can condensed cream of celery soup
185g (6^{1}/$_{2}$oz) can tuna chunks, drained
50g (2oz) red Leicester cheese, grated
2 tablespoons dry breadcrumbs
salt and freshly ground black pepper

You will also need a sharp knife, a cheese grater, a can opener, a wooden spoon, 3 large saucepans, a colander, a shallow heatproof bowl and oven gloves.

how do I do that?

1 Cook the cauliflower florets in boiling water for 5-10 minutes until just tender. Drain.

2 While the cauliflower is cooking, cook the macaroni following the packet instructions. Drain.

3 Melt the butter in the third large saucepan and fry the mushrooms until they are soft. Stir in the soup and cook over a low heat until it starts to bubble gently.

4 Stir in the cauliflower, macaroni, tuna and salt and pepper to taste. Preheat the grill to hot. Spoon the mixture into the shallow heatproof dish.

5 Sprinkle with the cheese and breadcrumbs and brown lightly under the grill. Carefully remove using oven gloves and serve at once.

three-cheese vegetable lasagne

A delicious and filling supper if you're called upon to cook!

what do I need?

45 mins — prep & cook time

serves 4

594 cals — per serving

22g fat — per serving

1 tablespoon olive oil

1 onion, sliced

2 courgettes, sliced

525g (1lb) jar of bolognese sauce

450g (15oz) natural cottage cheese

125g (4oz) mozzarella, grated

50g (2oz) fresh Parmesan or mature Cheddar cheese, finely grated

8 sheets dried egg lasagne or lasagne verdi

salt and freshly ground black pepper

You will also need a sharp knife, a cheese grater, a large saucepan, a wooden spoon, a mixing bowl and a 25 x 25cm (10 x 10in) lasagne dish.

how do I do that?

1 Heat the olive oil in the saucepan. Add the onion and courgettes and fry until softened but not browned. Stir in the bolognese sauce and add salt and pepper. Allow to simmer, uncovered, for 10 minutes.

2 Make the cheese topping. Mix together the cottage cheese, mozzarella and half of the Parmesan or Cheddar.

3 Preheat the oven to 200°C/400°F/gas mark 6. Lightly oil the lasagne dish. Spoon half the courgette sauce over the base of the dish and make level. Arrange 4 of the lasagne sheets over the top. Spoon over one half of the cheese mixture and spread it evenly.

4 Spoon over the rest of the courgette sauce and arrange the 4 remaining lasagne sheets on top. Spoon the remaining cheese mixture onto the lasagne and carefully smooth to the edges to cover evenly. Sprinkle over the remaining Parmesan or Cheddar.

5 Place the lasagne into the preheated oven for 30 minutes until it is golden brown and bubbling. Carefully remove from the oven using oven gloves and serve.

boston sausage & beans

Add a little zing to baked beans to make a special teatime treat.

what do I need?

30 mins
prep &
cook time

serves 6

337 cals
per
serving

17g fat
per
serving

50g (2oz) bacon, chopped

1/2 tablespoon mild curry powder

400g (13oz) can baked beans

375g (12oz) pork sausages, cooked, or any other favourite sausages

300g (10oz) ready-cooked rice

You will also need a sharp knife, a can opener, a wooden spoon and a medium saucepan.

how do I do that?

1 In the medium saucepan, fry the bacon over a moderate heat for 3-4 minutes. Add the curry powder and cook for a further minute, stirring occasionally.

2 Add the beans, turn down the heat and simmer for 6-8 minutes. Add the cooked sausages and cook for a further minute.

3 Heat the rice according to the instructions on the pack and divide between 6 plates, spooning the beans and sausages over the rice. Serve at once.

chicken & vegetable korma

45 mins
prep & cook time

serves 5

644 cals
per serving

16g fat
per serving

This is as good as any takeaway - serve with naan bread if you're especially hungry.

what do I need?

2 tablespoons oil

4 skinless chicken breasts, cut into bite-size pieces

2 x 260g (9oz) jars korma mild curry sauce

375g (12oz) broccoli, broken into florets, cooked and refreshed

2 sweet potatoes, peeled and cut into bite-size pieces

200g (7oz) basmati rice

1 x 20g ($^3/_4$oz) pack coriander, finely chopped (optional)

You will also need a sharp knife, a wooden spoon and 2 saucepans.

how do I do that?

1 Heat the oil in one of the saucepans, then add the chicken and cook for 4-5 minutes, stirring frequently, until it is lightly browned.

2 Stir in the curry sauce, bring to the boil and simmer gently over a low to moderate heat for 15 minutes, stirring occasionally. Add the broccoli and sweet potato and cook for 4-5 minutes.

3 In the meantime cook the basmati rice following the instructions on the pack.

4 Sprinkle the cooked curry with chopped coriander, if using, and serve with the rice.

Chop the coriander as shown on page 17, if using.

To cook and refresh broccoli - break the broccoli into small pieces. Bring a large pan of salted water to the boil, add the broccoli and cook for 3-5 minutes until just tender and still bright green. Drain the broccoli and run under cold water to stop the cooking process and keep the colour bright.

chilli con carne tacos

Impress your friends with these tasty tacos.

what do I need?

30 mins — prep & cook time

serves 6

372 cals — per serving

21g fat — per serving

1 tablespoon oil
1 onion, peeled and finely chopped
1 clove garlic, crushed
2 tablespoons mild chilli powder
500g (1lb) extra-lean minced beef
400g (13oz) can chopped tomatoes
420g (14oz) can kidney beans, drained and rinsed
1 green pepper, deseeded and cut into 1cm (1/2in) pieces
1 red chilli, deseeded and finely chopped
1 tablespoon tomato purée
12 taco shells
salt and freshly ground black pepper

You will also need a sharp knife, a garlic crusher, a can opener, a large saucepan with a lid and a wooden spoon.

how do I do that?

1 Heat the oil in a saucepan, then add the onion and garlic and fry until softened but not browned. Add the chilli powder and cook for a further minute.

2 Add the mince and cook until browned all over, stirring occasionally. Then stir in the chopped tomatoes, kidney beans, pepper, chilli and tomato purée. Cover and simmer for 30 minutes, stirring every now and then. Add salt and pepper to taste.

3 Heat the taco shells following the instructions on the pack then fill them with the chilli con carne and serve straightaway.

Add shredded lettuce, guacamole and sour cream or natural yogurt for extra garnish.

beef & bean pie

Crushed crisps make a crunchy topping for this tasty pie.

what do I need?

1 tablespoon vegetable oil
1 large onion, peeled and chopped
500g (1lb) lean minced beef
420g (14oz) can baked beans
2 tablespoons double concentrated tomato purée
300ml (10fl oz) beef stock, made from a beef stock cube made up in
    a jug with 300ml (10fl oz) boiling water
1 tablespoon Worcestershire sauce
2 x 25g (1oz) bags crisps, crushed to pieces
salt and freshly ground pepper

You will also need a sharp knife, a large saucepan, a wooden spoon, a
can opener, a heatproof jug and an ovenproof dish or individual dishes.

how do I do that?

1 Preheat the oven to 190°C/350°F/gas mark 5. Heat the oil in the
saucepan and fry the onion for 2-3 minutes until it is softened but
not browned. Add the mince to the pan and cook for 5 minutes,
stirring occasionally until the meat is brown all over.

2 Add the baked beans, tomato purée, stock and Worcestershire
sauce. Stir and cook for 15 minutes at a gentle bubble. Add salt and
pepper to taste.

3 Pour the mince mixture into the ovenproof dish or individual
dishes and sprinkle with the crushed crisps. Place in the oven for
10-15 minutes or until the crisps are lightly golden. Serve with
broccoli or spinach.

**Crush the crisps while they are still in the bag - just be careful
not to pop the bag and shower crumbs all over the kitchen.**

pasta with chicken and tomato sauce

This feel-good feast is guaranteed to fill you up!

what do I need?

150g (5oz) pasta shells
1 x 190g (7oz) jar tomato pasta sauce
75g (3oz) canned sweetcorn, drained
50g (2oz) frozen peas, cooked
150g (5oz) cooked chicken, cubed
50g (2oz) Cheddar cheese, grated

You will also need a sharp knife, a can opener, a wooden spoon, a saucepan, a cheese grater and a heatproof serving dish

how do I do that?

1 Cook the pasta shells for approximately 10-15 minutes until al dente, following the instructions on the pack.

2 Place the cooked pasta in a saucepan with the tomato sauce, sweetcorn, peas and cooked chicken. Stir well to combine and heat through thoroughly until piping hot.

3 Preheat the grill to hot. Spoon the mixture into the heatproof serving dish, sprinkle over the cheese and place under the grill for 2-3 minutes until the cheese is golden. Carefully remove using oven gloves, and allow to cool slightly before serving.

30
mins

285
cals

7g
fat

prep &
cook time

serves
3-4

per
serving

per
serving

Pasta should be cooked until it is 'al dente' which means cooked through, without being overcooked. It should still have a slight 'bite' when you chomp it rather than being mushy and too soft.

spanish omelette

Olé! Try this delicious Spanish speciality.

what do I need?

1 tablespoon oil

1 clove garlic, crushed

2 onions, sliced

125g (4oz) sweetcorn, drained or defrosted

1 medium potato, peeled, boiled and cut into bite-size pieces

50g (2oz) frozen peas

50g (2oz) chorizo or garlic sausage, finely chopped

8 medium-size eggs

2 tablespoons water

25g (1oz) butter

salt and freshly ground black pepper

You will also need a sharp knife, a garlic crusher, a frying pan, a wooden spoon, a spatula and 2 large bowls.

how do I do that?

30 mins — prep & cook time

serves 4-6

359 cals — per serving

22g fat — per serving

1 Heat the oil in the frying pan, add the garlic and onions and cook over a medium heat for 10 minutes until softened but not browned.

2 Mix the sweetcorn, potatoes, peas and sausage together in one of the bowls. Add the onions and garlic.

3 In the other bowl, beat the eggs together with the water and add salt and pepper to taste. Stir in the vegetable and sausage mixture until it is coated with the egg.

4 Melt the butter in a large frying pan. When it's sizzling, pour in the omelette mixture and cook over a medium heat for 5 minutes or until set, drawing the cooked edges towards the centre with a spatula or wooden spoon during the first minute.

5 Cut into thick slices and turn out onto warmed serving plates. Serve immediately.

If you like you can add a 100g (3¹/₂oz) can of drained and sliced sweet peppers (pimientos) to the vegetable and sausage mixture.

When you have melted the butter, add the egg mixture and swirl it around the pan, drawing the cooked bits round the edge towards the middle.

all-american hamburgers

| 30 mins | | 255 cals | 11g fat |
| prep & cook time | makes 4 burgers | per serving | per serving |

Everybody loves this state-side feast!

what do I need?

450g (1lb) minced beef
1 small onion, finely chopped
1 tablespoon chopped parsley
1 teaspoon salt
2 teaspoons Worcestershire sauce
4 hamburger buns
1 gherkin, sliced lengthways
½ small onion, thinly sliced
freshly ground black pepper

You will also need a sharp knife, a large mixing bowl and oven gloves.

how do I do that?

1 Mix the beef, onion, parsley, salt, Worcestershire sauce and black pepper to taste in the large bowl until thoroughly combined. Divide into 4 portions and shape each into a flat round about 2cm (3/4in) thick. Cook under a preheated hot grill for 5-6 minutes on each side. Carefully remove using oven gloves.

2 Slice the buns in half and place a hamburger on the bottom half of each. Top with a few slices of gherkin and onion and cover with the top half of the bun. Serve with corn relish or tomato sauce.

If you prefer, you can toast the buns before topping with a burger

chicken and pepperoni pizza

45 mins prep & cook time · serves 8 · **332 cals** per serving · **11g fat** per servin

Once you've made these tasty pizzas why not try making your own toppings?

what do I need?

300g (10oz) pack pizza base mix
1 tablespoon flour
300g (10oz) tub fresh tomato sauce
1 medium courgette, thinly sliced
375g (12oz) cooked chicken, cubed
125g (4oz) sliced pepperoni
4 ripe tomatoes, cut into quarters and the cores removed
2 tablespoons dried oregano
175g (6oz) mozzarella, grated
salt and freshly ground black pepper

You will also need a sharp knife, a large bowl, a cheese grater, a baking tray and oven gloves.

how do I do that?

1 Preheat the oven to 220°C/425°F/gas mark 7. Grease the baking tray.

2 Make up the pizza base mix in the large bowl following the instructions on the pack.

3 Divide the mixture into 8 equal balls and roll out on a floured surface into 12cm (5in) circles, then place on the greased baking tray.

4 Cover each base with 1 heaped tablespoon of tomato sauce and arrange the courgettes, cooked chicken, pepperoni and 2 pieces of tomato. Vary the toppings as you like.

5 Sprinkle with the oregano, season with salt and freshly ground black pepper and cover with the grated mozzarella.

6 Leave to stand for 10 minutes before placing on the top shelf of the oven for 15-20 minutes or until the cheese is bubbling and the crust is brown. Carefully remove from the oven using oven gloves. Leave the pizzas to rest for 2 minutes before eating.

For an extra-quick pizza, cheat and use a ready-prepared pizza base.

turkey kebabs

Kebabs on celery sticks - so you can even eat the kebab stick!

what do I need?

1/2 small onion, chopped
1 small courgette, grated
1 red pepper, deseeded and cubed
2 rashers bacon, chopped
375g (13oz) turkey mince
1 medium-size egg
100g (3^{1}/$_{2}$oz) breadcrumbs
4 sticks of celery, cut lengthways into 3
3 tablespoons vegetable oil

You will also need a cheese grater, a medium-sized mixing bowl and a non-stick frying pan.

how do I do that?

1 Mix the onion, courgette and red pepper in the bowl.

2 In the non-stick frying pan, cook the bacon without oil over a medium heat for 2-3 minutes and then add it to the bowl. Add the turkey mince, egg and breadcrumbs to the bowl and mix well.

3 Take a small handful of the mixture and 1 length of celery and gradually work the mixture around the celery, leaving a little celery exposed at each end so that you can hold it while eating. Repeat this until the mixture is used up. You should have 12 small kebabs.

4 Fry the kebabs in 3 batches (adding a tablespoon of oil for each batch), for 4-6 minutes on each side, turning frequently until golden and cooked through. Serve at once.

treasure island

1½ hrs
prep & cook time

serves 4

342 cals
per serving

13g fat
per serving

Set sail m' hearties to this edible island!

what do I need?

4 medium baking potatoes
425g (14oz) can minced beef
25g (1oz) butter
75g (3oz) sweetcorn, drained or defrosted
4 sticks celery with leafy top
1 tablespoon beef gravy granules

You will also need a small saucepan, a sharp knife, a potato masher, a medium-size bowl, a heatproof jug and oven gloves.

how do I do that?

1 Preheat the oven to 200°C/400°F/gas mark 6. Prick the baking potatoes all over with a fork and cook in the oven for approximately 1 hour or until soft. Heat the minced beef in the saucepan until hot.

2 Slice the top of the potato lengthways until it opens like a book. (Take care, as it will be very hot.) Scoop out the potato, mash it in the bowl with butter, then put to one side.

3 Fill the potato shell with the mince. Pile up the potato on a plate and plant the celery to resemble a palm tree. Place the potato on the mash and fill to overflowing with sweetcorn.

4 Make up the gravy according to the instructions on the pack and pour around the base of the 'island'.

turkey, ham & vegetable ribbons

25 mins
prep & cook time

serves 4

281 cals
per serving

14g fat
per serving

Everybody will love this colourful bowl of deliciousness!

what do I need?

250g (8oz) fresh tagliatelle
2 carrots, peeled and prepared as shown below
1 courgette, prepared as shown below
100g (3½oz) sliced ham, cut into strips
100g (3½oz) cooked sliced turkey, cut into strips
300g (10oz) fresh tomato and mascarpone sauce

You will also need a potato peeler, a large saucepan, a colander and a wooden spoon.

how do I do that?

1 Cook the tagliatelle and the carrot and courgette ribbons in lightly salted boiling water for 4 minutes and drain. Return the cooked, drained pasta and vegetables to the saucepan.

2 Add the ham, turkey and tomato and mascarpone sauce.

3 Heat through over a low heat, stirring occasionally, and serve.

Use the potato peeler to shave off long ribbons of carrot and courgette.

buried treasure

20 mins
prep & cook time

serves 4

232 cals
per serving

9g fat
per serving

Dig for the extra goodness in this delicious dish!

what do I need?

125g (4oz) cous cous
1 tablespoon olive oil
1 red onion, finely chopped
1 red or yellow pepper, finely chopped
125g (4oz) frozen peas, cooked
200g (7oz) salmon fillet, cooked and flaked

You will also need a sharp knife, a large heatproof bowl, a saucepan, a wooden spoon and a small bowl.

how do I do that?

1 Place the cous cous in the large bowl, cover with boiling water and leave to stand for 5 minutes, following the instructions on the pack.

2 Meanwhile heat the olive oil in the saucepan, add the onion and cook for 5 minutes, stirring occasionally. Add the pepper and cook for a further 2 minutes until the onion and pepper are softened but not browned.

3 When the cous cous is ready, stir it into the onion mixture. Add the peas and the salmon and stir to mix well.

This recipe is delicious hot or cold.

super side dishes

french beans in tomato sauce

These tasty beans will go perfectly with your favourite main course.

what do I need?

2 teaspoons corn oil
1 medium onion, peeled and chopped
2 cloves garlic, peeled and crushed
200g (7oz) can tomatoes, drained and chopped
1 teaspoon mixed herbs
1 tablespoon tomato purée
375g (12oz) French beans, topped and tailed
freshly ground black pepper

You will also need a sharp knife, a small saucepan, a garlic crusher and
a medium saucepan.

how do I do that?

1 Gently heat the oil in the small saucepan and fry the onion and
garlic until softened but not browned.

2 Add the tomatoes, herbs and tomato purée and cook over a low
heat at a gentle bubble for 15 minutes until it becomes thick.

3 Rinse the beans and cook them for 4 minutes in boiling salted
water in the medium saucepan, then drain.

4 Add salt and pepper to the tomato sauce and toss in the beans.
Raise the heat for half a minute and serve immediately.

30 mins
prep &
cook time

serves 6

50 cals
per
serving

2g fat
per
serving

courgette & tomato salad

30 mins
prep & cook time

serves 6

147 cals
per serving

10g fat
per serving

This hot salad is great with chicken, sausages or kebabs.

what do I need?

2 large onions, chopped
4 tablespoons oil
2 cloves garlic, crushed
1 teaspoon ground cumin
500g (1lb) courgettes, thickly sliced
2 tablespoons wine vinegar
a good pinch cayenne pepper, optional
500g (1lb) tomatoes, peeled and chopped
salt and freshly ground black pepper

You will also need a garlic crusher, a sharp knife, a saucepan and a fork or potato masher

how do I do that?

1 Fry the onion in the oil until softened but not browned. Add the garlic and cumin and stir.

2 Add the courgettes, salt, pepper, vinegar, cayenne, if using, and the tomatoes.

3 Put the lid on, and leave to steam over a low heat for about 10 minutes or until the courgettes are very tender.

4 Mash lightly with the fork or potato masher.

disco
light dips

30 mins
prep & cook time

serves 6-8

92 cals
per serving

8g fat
per serving

These colourful dips will add sparkle to any party!

what do I need?

150g (5oz) creamery soft cheese
1 tablespoon fresh pesto sauce
1/2 small green pepper, cored, deseeded and finely cubed
1/2 teaspoon paprika
1/2 small yellow pepper, cored, deseeded and finely cubed
1 tablespoon tomato purée or sundried tomato paste
1/2 small red pepper, cored, deseeded and finely cubed
1 pack mixed vegetable crudités

You will also need a sharp knife and 3 small bowls.

how do I do that?

1 Divide the soft cheese between 3 small bowls. Into the first one mix the pesto and green pepper, to the second add the paprika and yellow pepper, and to the last bowl add the tomato purée or paste and red pepper.

2 Serve the dips in a line to resemble disco lights and serve with the mixed crudités.

Crudités are raw vegetables used as dippers - use carrot and cucumber batons, cauliflower florets or strips of red or yellow pepper for a colourful display.

martian mash

30 mins — prep & cook time

456 cals — per serving

21g fat — per servin

serves 4-6

Eat it if you dare!

what do I need?

1.5kg (3½lb) potatoes, peeled and roughly chopped
250ml (8fl oz) milk
50g (2oz) butter
400g (13oz) fresh spinach, washed and patted dry
250g (8oz) Cheddar cheese, grated, and a little more to decorate
pinch freshly grated nutmeg
salt and freshly ground black pepper

You will also need a potato peeler, a cheese grater, 2 large saucepans, a potato masher and a food processor or hand-held blender.

how do I do that?

1 Cook the potatoes in boiling salted water for 10-15 minutes until soft. When cooked, drain and mash with the potato masher.

2 In the other saucepan, heat the milk and butter until the butter melts then add the spinach and cook for 1 minute.

3 Liquidise the spinach mixture, either in the pan with a hand-held blender, or in a food processor. You may have to do this in batches, depending on the size of your food processor, liquidising a little at a time and returning the liquidised mixture to the pan.

4 Add in the mashed potatoes and cheese and stir over a moderate heat until smooth. Season to taste and serve immediately.

Always make sure the lid of the food processor is firmly closed before you turn the machine on!

pirate boats

1½ hrs
prep & cook time

serves 4

228 cals
per serving

5g fat
per serving

Set sail for a hearty meal!

what do I need?

2 baking potatoes
4 cheese slices
1 carrot, peeled and cut into 8 long thin sticks
8 cherry tomatoes
150g (5oz) petits pois

You will also need a baking tray, a sharp knife and oven gloves.

how do I do that?

1 Preheat the oven to 200°C/400°F/gas mark 6.

2 Prick the potatoes all over with a fork, place on the baking tray and cook for approximately 1 hour or until soft.

3 Carefully cut the cooked potatoes in half lengthways. (Take care, as they will be very hot.)

4 Cut each cheese slice into two and thread one half on to each of the carrot sticks to resemble a mast. Stand one carrot stick up in each potato boat. Cut the cherry tomatoes in half and push one half on to the top of each potato as a cabin.

5 Serve the boats on a 'sea' of petits pois or other favourite vegetable.

20 mins
prep & cook time

serves 4

228 cals
per serving

9g fat
per serving

jewelled egg rice

This delicious and colourful rice dish is great with chicken or sausages.

what do I need?

4 medium eggs
1 tablespoon milk
10g (½oz) butter
125g (4oz) long-grain rice, boiled and drained
50g (2oz) sweetcorn, drained or defrosted
50g (2oz) frozen peas, cooked

You will also need a small mixing bowl, a balloon whisk, a non-stick saucepan and a wooden spoon.

how do I do that?

1 Crack the eggs into the bowl, add the milk and beat together.

2 Melt the butter in the saucepan, add the egg mixture and cook over a medium heat for about 5 minutes, stirring continually until lightly scrambled.

3 Add the rice, sweetcorn and peas to the scrambled egg mixture. Heat through, stirring occasionally, and serve straight away.

If you like, you can serve with bread 'soldiers' as we have done.

curly cabbage & new potato nests

30 mins
prep & cook time

serves 6

128 cals
per serving

3g fat
per serving

Nothing beats the flavour of baby new potatoes - even better with a little melted butter!

what do I need?

750g (1½lb) baby new potatoes, cut in half if large
1 savoy cabbage, shredded
25g (1oz) butter

You will also need a sharp knife, 2 large saucepans and a colander.

how do I do that?

1 Cook the new potatoes in lightly salted boiling water for 15-20 minutes, until just tender.

2 Meanwhile, steam or boil the cabbage for 10-12 minutes until 'al dente'.

3 Drain the cabbage and arrange on a serving plate to form a 'nest'. Place the potatoes in the centre as 'eggs', and serve with the butter melting over the potatoes.

'Al dente' means cooked through but not overcooked. The cabbage should still be firm when you bite into it. The same term is used for pasta.

fried sweetcorn

30 mins
prep & cook time

serves 4

114 cals
per serving

9g fat
per servin

This colourful side dish will liven up any meal!

what do I need?

2 tablespoons cooking oil

1/2 medium onion, finely chopped

1 green pepper, deseeded and cut in thin strips

4 tablespoons chopped parsley

1 chilli, deseeded and finely chopped, optional

375g (12oz) sweetcorn, drained or defrosted

125g (4oz) fresh mushrooms, sliced

1 chicken stock cube

freshly ground black pepper

You will also need a sharp knife and a frying pan with a lid.

how do I do that?

1 Heat the oil in the frying pan and fry the onion, pepper, parsley and chilli, if using, until the onion is softened but not browned.

2 Add the sweetcorn and mushrooms and crumble the stock cube over the top. Stir, cover with a lid, and cook over a medium heat for 5 minutes. Uncover and continue frying for 5 minutes more, stirring frequently. Serve hot, sprinkled with a pinch of black pepper.

cheesy rice

20 mins
prep & cook time

serves 4

319 cals
per serving

10g fat
per serving

It just couldn't be simpler to make this cheesily delicious side dish!

what do I need?

200g (7oz) long-grain rice, boiled and drained
125g (4oz) cheese spread

You will also need a large saucepan, a colander, a large bowl and a wooden spoon.

how do I do that?

1 Drain the cooked rice and turn out into the large bowl.

2 Stir the cheese spread through the rice, stirring well to make sure it is thoroughly mixed.

3 Serve straight away.

This is especially good served with fish fingers, salmon, chicken or vegetables.

sweet eats

sticky cornflake flapjack

A deliciously sticky treat to slip into your lunchbox or to eat after school when hunger pangs strike.

what do I need?

75g (3oz) unsalted butter

75g (3oz) light muscovado sugar

50g (2oz) syrup

50g (2oz) oats

50g (2oz) cornflakes

50g (2oz) desiccated coconut

50g (2oz) ready-to-eat pineapple, finely chopped

You will also need a 20 x 20cm (8 x 8in) shallow baking tin, a large saucepan, a wooden spoon, a knife, oven gloves and a wire cooling rack.

how do I do that?

1 Preheat the oven to 180°C/350°F/gas mark 4. Grease the baking tin.

2 In the large pan, melt the butter, sugar and syrup over a moderate heat.

3 Using the wooden spoon, carefully stir in the remaining ingredients. Mix well to coat the dry ingredients thoroughly with the butter and sugar mixture.

4 Spoon the mixture into the baking tin and press down well with the back of the spoon so that the surface is level.

30 mins
prep & cook time

makes 12 pieces

140 cals
per serving

8g fat
per serving

5 Bake for 10-15 minutes in the preheated oven.

6 Carefully remove from the oven using oven gloves and score into pieces with the tip of a knife. Leave to set, then carefully remove the pieces from the tin and leave to cool thoroughly on a wire rack.

milk lollies

3 hrs
prep time

makes 12
lollies

32 cals
per serving

1g fat
per serving

These banana lollies are delicious, but you could use strawberries or any other favourite soft fruit.

what do I need?

150ml (5fl oz) milk
150g (5oz) carton natural yogurt
1 ripe banana, peeled
2 teaspoons clear honey

You will also need a food processor and 12 lolly moulds.

how do I do that?

Place all the ingredients in a food processor or blender and process for 20 seconds until smooth.

Pour into the lolly moulds and freeze for 3 hours, until solid.

Always make sure the lid of the food processor is firmly closed before you turn the machine on!

chocolate dip

Who could resist this delicious dip?

what do I need?

1/2 x 400g (13oz) jar chocolate spread, gently warmed
4 tablespoons milk or single cream
6-8 marshmallows
2 kiwi fruit, peeled and quartered
10 strawberries, leaves removed and halved
1 banana, peeled and cut into chunks
2 peaches or nectarines, stoned and cut into wedges
1 small pineapple, peeled, cored and cut into wedges

You will also need a sharp knife, a balloon whisk, a serving bowl and skewers.

how do I do that?

1 Whisk together the chocolate spread and milk or single cream. Transfer to a small warmed serving bowl and place in the centre of a large serving plate.

2 Skewer the marshmallows and prepared fruit and place on the table for everyone to help themselves.

Don't prepare the fruit too far in advance or it may turn brown and many of the vitamins will be lost.

Melting chocolate or chocolate spread in a bowl over a pan of hot water stops it from overheating and spoiling.

strawberry milk jelly

2 hrs
prep time

serves 6

172 cals
per serving

6g fat
per serving

A dreamy dessert that's really fun to make.

what do I need?

135g (4¹/₂oz) pack of strawberry flavour jelly
150ml (5fl oz) boiling water
410g (13oz) can evaporated milk
250g (8oz) fresh strawberries, leaves removed, and sliced

You will also need a heatproof bowl, a large mixing bowl, an electric hand whisk and a large serving dish or 6 small serving dishes.

how do I do that?

1 Dissolve the jelly in the boiling water and allow to cool.

2 Pour the evaporated milk into the large bowl and whisk with the electric hand whisk for 6-8 minutes until the mixture is light and fluffy and leaves a trail.

3 Whisk in the cooled jelly and pour into a serving dish or 6 individual serving dishes. Place in a refrigerator for 1-2 hours to set and serve topped with the sliced strawberries.

banana
and grape brûlée

30 mins — prep & cook time

serves 4

205 cals — per serving

6g fat — per servir

The crisp and crunchy topping makes this dessert extra brilliant.

what do I need?

2 bananas, sliced
12 seedless grapes, halved
250ml (9fl oz) Greek yogurt
425ml (15fl oz) custard
sugar for sprinkling

You will also need a sharp knife, 4 individual heatproof dishes, a medium mixing bowl and oven gloves.

how do I do that?

1 Divide the bananas and grapes between the 4 dishes.

2 Mix the yogurt and custard together in the mixing bowl and the spoon it over the fruit.

3 Preheat the grill to hot.

4 Sprinkle each ramekin quite thickly with sugar and carefully plac under the grill until the sugar melts and turns brown. It will be very hot so take care. Chill briefly and serve.

Try using other fruit, such as kiwi fruit, cubes of melon or satsuma segments. You can also use canned fruit in juice if you prefer.

currant bun, fruit & yogurt breakfast

We all know that breakfast is the most important meal of the day – well, here's one that will get you off to a good start in the morning.

what do I need?

3 medium-size eggs, beaten

150ml (5fl oz) milk

pack of 4 currant buns

2 teaspoons butter

2 peaches, nectarines or kiwi fruit, sliced

25g (1oz) black seedless grapes

25g (1oz) white seedless grapes

125g (4oz) strawberries, hulled

2 bananas, peeled and sliced

300g (10oz) tub natural Greek yogurt

1 tablespoon clear honey (optional)

You will also need a knife, a large shallow dish, a balloon whisk and a frying pan.

how do I do that?

1 Beat together the egg and milk in the shallow dish. Add the currant buns in one layer and leave for a few minutes to soak up the egg mixture, turning occasionally to coat evenly .

2 Heat the butter in the frying pan, add the currant buns and fry for 1-2 minutes each side over a moderate heat until golden all over. Remove from the pan and cut into squares.

3 Divide the fruit and yogurt between the serving dishes, top with the currant bun squares and drizzle over the honey, if using. Yum!

apricot whip

A fresh and fruity dessert that's ready in minutes.

what do I need?

125g (4oz) ready-to-eat dried apricots
6 tablespoons orange juice
150g (5oz) carton natural yogurt
250ml (9fl oz) ready-made fresh custard

You will also need a medium saucepan, a blender and 4 serving dishes.

how do I do that?

1 Place the apricots in the saucepan with the orange juice and cook gently over a low heat for 2 minutes. Remove from the heat and allow to cool.

2 Place the fruit and juice in the blender with the yogurt and custard and blend until smooth. Spoon into the serving dishes or glasses and put in the fridge to chill for 15 minutes before serving.

Use ready-to-eat vanilla prunes or other favourite dried fruit instead of apricots to make a delicious variation of this recipe.

muddy puddles

 10 mins
prep & cook time

 serves 4

 332 cals
per serving

11g fat
per servin

Make a splash with this tasty pudding.

what do I need?

425g (14oz) can creamed rice pudding
1 teaspoon cocoa powder
50g (2oz) dried, ready-to-eat apricots, chopped
50g (2oz) sultanas

You will also need a can opener, a sharp knife, a mixing bowl, a wooden spoon and 4 serving bowls.

how do I do that?

1 Empty the rice pudding into the bowl and stir in the cocoa, apricots and sultanas.

2 Serve in 4 individual bowls to make muddy puddles!

I'm thirsty!

hot chocolate and banana milkshake

Scrumptiously warming and full of goodness, this is the perfect treat for a cold winter's day.

what do I need?

15 mins — prep & cook time
serves 4
252 cals — per serving
12g fat — per serving

1 litre (1³/₄ pints) whole or
   semi-skimmed milk
2 large ripe bananas, peeled and roughly chopped
50g (2oz) plain chocolate drops
4 cinnamon sticks, optional, or chocolate flakes

You will also need a measuring jug, a knife, a large non-stick saucepan, a wooden spoon and a hand-held electric blender.

how do I do that?

1 Put the milk, bananas, and chocolate in the saucepan over a low heat. Slowly bring to the boil, stirring occasionally.

2 Take the pan off the heat and use a hand-held blender to blend the mixture thoroughly until it is frothy and smooth.

3 Pour into 4 mugs and add a cinnamon stick to each one.

Make sure you keep stirring to stop the mixture sticking to the bottom of the pan, otherwise it will burn.

Take the pan off the heat and put it on a heat proof non-slip surface before you use the hand-held blender to make the mixture smooth and frothy.

watermelon crush

10 mins
prep time

serves 2

52 cals
per serving

1g fat
per serving

This cooling drink is bound to become a summertime favourite.

what do I need?

250g (8oz) slice watermelon
3 tablespoons blackcurrant drink
300ml (10fl oz) water
2 ice cubes

You will also need a sharp knife, a food processor or blender, 2 glasses and some straws, if you like.

how do I do that?

1 Carefully cut off the skin of the watermelon. Use a teaspoon to scoop out the seeds. Chop the flesh into chunks.

2 Place in the food processor or blender with all the rest of the ingredients and blend for 15-20 seconds until smooth.

3 Pour into glasses and serve immediately.

Always make sure the lid of the blender is firmly closed before you turn the machine on!

For a change, add a few strawberries or raspberries when you put the ingredients in the blender.

apple and strawberry fizz

This fizzy drink is perfect for pouring out for friends on a hot summer's day in the garden.

what do I need?

prep time

serves 6

74
cals
per
serving

0g
fat
per
serving

½ x 20g (³/₄oz) pack mint, leaves
  removed from the stems
1 litre (1³/₄ pints) apple & strawberry juice
150ml (5fl oz) sparkling water
1 red-skinned dessert apple, sliced

You will also need an ice-cube tray, a sharp knife and a large
serving jug.

how do I do that?

1 Put the mint leaves in the ice-cube tray, add some water and
freeze for about 1 hour until solid.

2 Pour the apple and strawberry juice into the jug, followed by the
sparkling water.

3 Drop in the ice cubes and add the apple slices to decorate.

**Make the ice-cubes in advance and leave them in the freezer.
You can make more of them than you need for this recipe and
use them in other drinks as well.**

**If you don't have an apple, you could decorate this drink with
strawberries or other fruit instead.**

strawberry & banana smoothie

10 mins prep time

serves 3-4

91 cals per serving

1g fat per serving

Smoothies are fun to make and full of goodness.

what do I need?

250g (8oz) punnet strawberries, leaves removed
1 medium banana, peeled and roughly chopped
300ml (10fl oz) semi-skimmed milk
150ml (5fl oz) natural yogurt
1 tablespoon runny honey

You will also need a sharp knife, a measuring jug and a food processor or blender.

how do I do that?

1 Simply put all the above ingredients into a food processor, blender or smoothie maker. Blend until smooth.

2 Adjust the sweetness, adding a little more honey if you have a sweet tooth, and pour into serving glasses.

Always make sure the lid of the food processor is firmly closed before you turn the machine on!

You can replace the strawberries with the same weight of peeled kiwi fruit or raspberries or other soft fruit if you prefer.

pineapple yogurt shake

A fruity milkshake that's extra-quick to prepare.

what do I need?

450g (15oz) can of pineapple pieces in juice
150g (5oz) natural yogurt
2 tablespoons clear honey (optional)

You will also need a can opener, a food processor or blender and 2 tall glasses.

how do I do that?

1 Place all the ingredients in a blender or food processor and blend until smooth.

2 Pour the mixture into 2 tall glasses and chill until ready to serve.

Always make sure the lid of the food processor is firmly closed before you turn the machine on!

It is better to use pineapple in juice, not syrup, for this recipe, as it contains less added sugar.

For a chunkier shake, just blend for a few seconds.

bake that!

hedgehog bread rolls

2 hrs
prep & cook time

makes 8 rolls

243 cals
per serving

3g fat
per servin

These spiky critters taste delicious!

what do I need?

500g (1lb) white bread flour
1 teaspoon salt
1 sachet easy-blend dried yeast
1 tablespoon sunflower oil
250ml (8fl oz) lukewarm water
extra flour, for dusting
extra oil, for brushing
16 currants, optional

You will also need a sieve, a large bowl, a wooden spoon, some cling film, a knife and a pair of kitchen scissors, a lightly-oiled baking tray, oven gloves and a wire cooling rack.

how do I do that?

1 Sieve the flour into the bowl with the salt and yeast. Make a large well in the centre. Spoon in the oil and pour in almost all the water. Mix the oil and water into the flour with a large wooden spoon until the dough is soft but not sticky. If it's too dry, add a little more wate

2 Turn the dough onto a lightly floured surface and knead it for 8-10 minutes until you have a smooth, springy dough ball. Put it bac in the mixing bowl.

3 Tear off a sheet of cling film large enough to cover the bowl.

Brush it lightly with oil, then cover the bowl with it, oiled side down. Leave the dough in a warm place for at least an hour until it has doubled in size. Take it out of the bowl and knead it again as you did before, but only for a minute or two this time.

4 Cut the dough into 8 pieces. Shape into animal shapes, or into plain bread rolls if you prefer. To make hedgehog shapes as shown, shape the dough into balls. Pull out one end to make a snout, stick currants on for eyes, and use small scissors to snip the top into peaks. Preheat the oven to 200°C/400°F/gas mark 6.

5 Place the rolls on the baking tray, cover with the cling film and leave them until they have doubled in size. Then remove the cling film and put the rolls in the preheated oven and bake for 12-15 minutes near the top of the oven until golden. Carefully remove using oven gloves. Cool on a wire rack.

apricot & oat fingers

These flavour-packed fingers are bursting with energy!

what do I need?

45 mins — prep & cook time

274 cals — per serving

16g fat — per serving

makes 14 pieces

250g (8oz) dried apricots, chopped
3 tablespoons apple juice
175ml (6fl oz) sunflower oil
4 tablespoons clear honey
175g (6oz) porridge oats
150g (5oz) plain flour
50g (2oz) walnuts, chopped

You will also need a knife, a 20 x 20cm (8 x 8in) baking tin, a small saucepan, a medium saucepan, a wooden spoon, oven gloves and a knife

how do I do that?

1 Preheat the oven to 190°C/375°F/gas mark 5. Grease and line the baking tin.

2 Place the apricots and apple juice in the small saucepan and simmer over a low heat for 5 minutes until soft.

3 Place the oil and honey in the medium saucepan and stir over a low heat until evenly blended. Add the oats, flour and walnuts and mix together thoroughly. Put half the mixture into the baking tin and press down firmly with the back of the wooden spoon.

4 Cover with the apricot mixture, then sprinkle over the remaining oat mixture and press down firmly.

5 Bake for 35 minutes until golden brown. Remove from the oven with oven gloves and leave to cool for 5 minutes, then cut into 14 fingers. Allow to cool completely before removing from the tin.

gingerbread men

Everybody loves gingerbread men!

what do I need?

1½ hrs prep & cook time   makes 6   **280 cals** per serving   **11g fat** per serving

125g (4oz) unsalted butter
100g (3¹/₂oz) caster sugar
1 medium egg, beaten
3 tablespoons golden syrup
300g (10oz) plain flour
1 teaspoon bicarbonate of soda
5 teaspoons ground ginger
200g (7oz) fondant icing sugar
food colouring
writing icing tubes

You will also need a large baking tray, a wooden spoon or electric hand mixer, a large mixing bowl, a sieve, some cling film, a rolling pin, a gingerbread man cutter, oven gloves and a wire cooling rack.

how do I do that?

1 Grease the baking tray with oil or butter.

2 Cream the butter and sugar together until light and fluffy, using the wooden spoon or electric hand mixer. Beat in the egg and golden syrup and mix together well.

3 Sift the flour, bicarbonate of soda and ground ginger into the mixture. Mix into a smooth dough, wrap it with cling film, and put in the fridge to chill for at least 1 hour.

4 Preheat the oven to 180°C/350°F/gas mark 4. Roll out the dough to a thickness of 1cm (¹/₂in), and cut out using a gingerbread man pastry cutter. Place the gingerbread men on the baking tray, spaced well apart as they will spread slightly.

5 Bake for 8-10 minutes until golden brown, then carefully remove from the oven using oven gloves and allow to cool slightly. Transfer to a cooling rack to finish cooling.

6 Make some fondant icing by following the instructions on the pack of fondant icing sugar and stir in a few drops of food colouring. Use the fondant icing to decorate the gingerbread men and finish with the writing icing to give them eyes and mouths.

smashing scones

Fill with jam and cream for a tasty treat.

what do I need?

45 mins		**105** cals	**5g** fat
prep & cook time	makes 12 scones	per serving	per serving

125g (4oz) wholemeal stoneground flour
125g (4oz) self-raising flour, plus extra
  for dusting
1 teaspoon baking powder
good pinch of salt
75g (3oz) butter, cut into small pieces
approximately 150ml (5fl oz) milk

You will also need a baking tray, a large bowl, a sieve, pastry cutters, oven gloves and a wire cooling rack.

how do I do that?

1 Preheat the oven to 200°C/400°F/gas mark 6. Grease the baking tray with oil or butter.

2 Sift the flours, baking powder and salt into the bowl, and tip in any bran caught in the sieve. Add the butter and rub it into the flour using your fingertips until the mixture looks like breadcrumbs.

3 Mix in enough milk to form a soft dough; don't make it too firm a the flour will continue to absorb moisture and firm up while you work. Turn the dough onto a floured surface and knead it lightly.

4 Roll out the dough to a thickness of 1.5cm (3/4in). Using a 5cm (2in) cutter, cut out 12 scones, and place on the baking tray. Bake in the preheated oven for 15-20 minutes until golden and risen. Carefully remove using oven gloves and cool on a wire rack.

To serve, you can fill with your favourite jam and cream. The calories and fat figures refer to the scones before they are filled.

Roll out the dough to a thickness of about 1.5cm (¾in), then cut it out.

banana and honey muffins

These won't last long! A couple for breakfast are great!

what do I need?

40 mins prep & cook time

makes 12 muffins

167 cals per serving

5g fat per serving

250g (8oz) self-raising flour, sifted
25g (1oz) soft dark brown sugar
50g (2oz) butter, melted
2 small ripe bananas, mashed
2 medium-size eggs, beaten
2 tablespoons clear honey
5 tablespoooons milk
2 teaspoons clear honey
3 tablespoons icing sugar, sifted
few drops lemon juice

You will also need a bun tin and 12 paper cases, 2 large mixing bowls, a wooden spoon, a balloon whisk, oven gloves, a wire cooling rack and a small bowl.

how do I do that?

1 Preheat the oven to 200°C/400°F/gas mark 6. Place the bun cases in the bun tin.

2 Place the flour, sugar, butter and bananas in one of the large bowls and mix them together.

3 In the second bowl, whisk together the eggs, honey and milk and beat into the other ingredients to form a mixture of soft dropping consistency.

4 Divide the mixture between the cases, filling almost to the top.

5 Bake in the preheated oven for approximately 15 minutes until risen and firm to the touch. Carefully remove from the oven using oven gloves then transfer to a wire rack to cool.

6 To make the icing, mix together the honey, icing sugar and lemon juice and place a little on top of each muffin.

To make the bees, use black icing pen to make stripes on yellow jelly sweet. For the wings, cut a heart-shaped piece of rice paper, outline in black icing. Cut a little slit in the top of each 'bee' and insert the wings carefully.

special sponge cake

When it's your Mum's birthday, this makes the day into a special occasion.

what do I need?

175g (6oz) butter or margarine
75g (3oz) caster sugar
3 large eggs, lightly beaten
1 teaspoon vanilla extract
175g (6oz) self-raising flour
1 teaspoon baking powder
1 tablespoon hot water
200g (7oz) creamery light soft cheese
25g (1oz) icing sugar
1 teaspoon vanilla extract
fresh fruit of your choice, optional

45 mins
prep & cook time

serves 10

297 cals
per serving

12g fat
per serving

You will also need 2 x 17cm (7in) cake tins, greaseproof paper, a large mixing bowl, a wooden spoon or electric hand mixer, oven gloves, a wire cooling rack and a small bowl.

how do I do that?

1 Preheat the oven to 180°C/350°F/gas mark 4. Grease the cake tins with butter or oil then line them with greaseproof paper.

2 Cream together the butter and sugar until light and fluffy, using a wooden spoon or an electric hand mixer, and beat in the eggs, a little at a time, with the vanilla extract.

3 Fold in the flour, baking powder and hot water and mix well.

4 Spoon into the tins. Bake for 20 minutes, until they are well risen and firm to the touch.

5 Carefully remove from the oven using oven gloves and turn out onto the rack to cool.

6 To make the topping and filling, mix together the creamery soft cheese, icing sugar and vanilla extract in the small bowl until soft. Use half the mixture to sandwich the cakes together, with the fruit, if using, and spread the rest on top. Just before serving, decorate with the remaining fruit.

index